Finding My Way

Crystal Myers

BookLeaf
Publishing

Presentation by *BookLeaf Publishing*

Web: www.bookleafpub.com

E-mail: info@bookleafpub.com

ISBN : 9789357210232

First edition 2022

DEDICATION

To my two beautiful children Jada and Nina, my inspirations to keep pressing towards my goal, no matter what obstacles may come my way.

Insecure Me

For many years I struggled with the basics
Like staying true to myself no matter what the
case is
I've been a pleaser of people damn near my
whole life
Doing what others expected of me even when I
knew it wasn't right
Always second guessing my own decisions
Then ending up stuck
In this prison
Of my mind
Telling me thoughts that are unkind
Like I don't deserve the best
And the my life will always be a mess
But one day I decided to try something new
Something that required me to be true
Doing things for myself without feeling guilty
Taking care of my mind and my body carefully
Loving myself, flaws and all
Being honest with myself and standing tall
God has shown me His grace
And because of this fact
I will finish my race
I will show and give love freely
Because now I don't have to fake
I am finally free.

Distracted AF

Distractions are apart of life
There will always be something else to do
An option that seems better at the moment
But is really taking away from you
Taking away from your plans and dreams
Something that you could be doing to better
yourself
Instead of going along with nonsense schemes
And putting your dreams up on the shelf
When the distractions are gone
And there's nothing else to do
You're left feeling empty
Feeling like you can't make due
We get so caught up
In being there for others
We neglect ourselves
And those close to us
Distractions will come and
Distractions will go
The most important thing to remember
Is to prepare for your OWN tomorrow.

High hopes?

People often ask me
Why am I always so happy?
I think that it's because my hopes
Are higher than reality
They ask
How can I smile
When troubles are surrounding me?
It's because I know I'm loved
And I'm blessed by the Highest, see
Beginning to realize my worth
For the first time in forever
Has me questioning some things
Like how in the hell did I ever?
Did I ever not think more of myself
Was it out of desperation?
That I settled
For less than I deserved
Or was it out of fear
That I wouldn't receive better
Boy, I really had the nerve
Had the audacity to question God
To be impatient
Is that odd?
Odd to think that the best
Was so far out of my reach
Such a hypocrite

How can I not practice what I preach?
If I love to see others happy
And love to see them win
Why is it so hard for me
To see my own happy end?

A Breath of Fresh Air

A breath of fresh air
Without a worry nor care
Built to last, stand tall.

Playing it Safe

I too often play things safe
In fear of rejection
I often downplay my victories
To make others not feel out of place
The thing about playing my cards this way
Is that I will never reach my full potential
No how, no way
The only way to do life
Is to take a chance
On something that you normally wouldn't do
The most important thing
Is to stay true to you.

Under Pressure

Pressures all around me
Things that I cannot control
Head above water, steady wins the race.

Love Is…

Love is complex
Small word with such big meaning
It's not just about the sex
Or how big the ring is
Love is not just wanting
The best for yourself
It's about making sure your partners good
Above everyone else
Love is being their safe place
Someone who listens
Gives sound advice
So that there is less tension
You will disagree because the two are not the
same
But at the end of the day
The two should always remain
Synced with one another
On one accord
Knowing that nothing can break
The string with 3 cords.

Unapologetically Me

I used to try and hide behind
Different ideas and versions of myself
That I had outgrown so long ago
Trying to dim my own light
Because I didn't feel worthy enough
Strong enough
Brave enough
To shine
To grow
To leave everything behind
To trust that God will never take
What he can't upgrade or replace
I held onto things that hurt me
So much that I thought " I deserve that"
I held onto those I thought could be healed with
my love
Then to learn some hurts can only be healed
from God above
In the process of this growing pain
I've lost some things
But I've also gained
I gained truth, honesty, wisdom
Things that can't be caught on sale
These things have taught me
To love myself on a much larger scale
I'm fat

I'm funny
I'm witty
A lil nerdy too
I love to cook
I like to eat
I can be a b!@*# at times too
I can now love myself
Regardless of how others feel about me
Flaws and all
Here I am
Unapologetically me.

Taking Flight

Even if you're scared
You should try anyway
Resources seem limited?
Disregard the naysay
Be still enough to hear
The tiny voice inside you
The one that guides
Discerns and directs you
The funny thing about flights are
That they can be a little scary
But in order for you to get to the next place in
life
Flight is necessary.

Lost in the Sauce

In my journey I have found
That more often than not
There have been times when
All I've had to give is all that I got
In the middle of my personal storm
I am able to pull myself out for a few
To say hello, a few kind words
To someone who may also be going through
Smile on my face
Joy in my heart
Knowing that just because times are hard
Doesn't mean that they will last
Don't be ashamed of your shortcomings
Your imperfections or dysfunction
We are all just trying to figure life out
One day at a time.

God's Grace

That feeling that you get
When you rise in the morning
From the crack of your neck
To the long, loud yawning
His grace in our life is shown in the little things
Things we either take for granted
Or we really don't need
Grace is a gift that cannot be earned
Yet it is given all the same
Along with the ability to discern
So that we can sort out some things
He gives us this grace
So that we too can give it to others
To our coworkers, strangers
Sisters and brothers
Instead of condemning
We should be showing love
Then we all can truly begin the path
To be the change and start mending.

Nobody's Perfect

From the first glance that you share
Conversations that have been had
Nothing is quite as intense as
The way you make each other laugh
Simply enjoying one another's company
Making plans and holding hands
Thinking this could be the one
Then life takes a turn
Things aren't as smooth as they have once been
Troubles coming from all sides
But instead of giving in
Two people who have made a decision to love
To be loyal and cherish each other above
All and everyone else
Yes, at times they will be at odds
They will not always agree
But their saving grace is that they care for each
other without cause
Knowing that the other person is human
We can then accept each others flaws
And forgive them for their shortcomings
Then two can form an unstoppable union.

Say Yes

Say yes to your dreams
Even when you don't know where to start
Begin making a plan
And let your plan be guided by your heart
Say yes to the possibility of failing
Because at least you will have tried
And if it doesn't work out
Don't you dare run and hide
Say yes to round two
Rounds three and four
Because no matter what
You keep coming back for more
Staying consistent and positive
Wins the race
Doesn't matter if you're in first
Second or third place
You will have done your part
And gave it your best
All because you decided to
Say yes.

Blue Sky

Skies so blue, so calm
Gaze up in the sky, oh my
Beautiful day, lovely sky

The children are OUR future

Working at a middle school
And some ask me why
Am I crazy,is it worth it
Why do I even try
I respond that I must be crazy
To work in a profession as such
But the reason why I choose my job
It's because I love those damn kids so much
They can be challenging at times
Very mouthy and obscene
But the thing that brings me back to work
everyday
Is the fact that we are teaching these little human
beings
Yes, the job is stressful
And trying at times
But nothing is more rewarding
Than watching these kids grow and shine
Sometimes it feels like our tries are for naught
But everyday we all show up
And give it everything we got
Yes, we do at times fail
But do we give up on them
No way in hell
We strive to teach these kids not only their
studies

But how to get along
At school, at home, in life in general
Showing them the small things
That are so very meaningful
Children are our future
Yes, this is true
That's why we as educators
Do what it is we do.

No Can Do (Boundaries)

Boundaries are a
Necessity, nonetheless
So place yours wisely.

Self Love is Best

Loving myself is the best
But hardest thing that I have done to date
When people say they love themselves
I haven't always been able to relate
In the past, I've settled for less
Didn't always know that what I had to offer
Was the best
As I've grown and matured I've begun to learn
myself
I know now what to keep
And what to put back on the shelf
I also know that as long as I am chasing God
I will never again be in a stagnant state
Or against the odds
Loving myself is finally something with which I
can relate.

For my children

Mommy loves you
I hope that you know
I always want the best for you
Let me plant you so that you can grow
Grow to be the young women
I know that you can be
Learn the world for yourself
And set healthy boundaries
You are loved
You are beautiful
You are set apart
You are wise
You are spontaneous
You have a caring heart
We may have our times
When we don't see eye to eye
That's just apart of the journey
You will understand better by and by
Your mother loves you
I've loved you from the very start
And no matter what the case
I thank God that He placed you in my care and
in my heart.